THE TRUSTWORTHINESS
OF RELIGIOUS EXPERIENCE

The Trustworthiness
of
Religious Experience

by
D. Elton Trueblood

Friends United Press
Richmond, Indiana

LIBRARY OF CONGRESS
Library of Congress Cataloging-in-Publication Data

Trueblood, Elton, 1900-
        The trustworthiness of religious experience/ by D. Elton
Trueblood. — 2nd Friends United Press ed.
        p.   cm.
        Reprint. Originally published: London: Allen & Unwin, 1939. With
new pref.
        ISBN 0-944350-00-3
        1. Experience (Religion) 2. Knowledge, Theory of (Religion)
I. Title.
BL53.T73 1988
291.4'2 — dc19

First published in 1939 as a Swarthmore Lecture of London Yearly Meeting,
    Religious Society of Friends.
First Friends United Press edition 1979. Published by permission.

PREFACE

The rationality of Quaker thinking has always been empirical. The key word used in the connection by George Fox was "experimental," which may be seen as essentially the same as "experiential." This has been employed by Friends as contrary to whatever is merely speculative in belief. Friends, from the first, more than three hundred years ago, have emphasized not knowledge *about* God, but *direct experience* of His presence in their lives.

With this critical point in mind, I determined , when asked to give the Swarthmore Lecture in London, in 1939, to deal with the crucial issue of whether direct religious experience can be trusted. I was determined to raise the question of credibility in a mood akin to that which marks natural science. When persons report a direct experience of God by acquaintance, are they dealing with what is objective and real, or are they merely enjoying their own fantasies?

In approaching this subject I employed the same logic to which I had recently been introduced in my graduate studies at Johns Hopkins University. I was convinced then, as I am convinced now, that epistemology is the central discipline of philosophy, and that it can be applied to religious experience in the same way that it is applied to sensory experience. The objects of study are different, but the essential method is the same.

One reason for selecting this subject of inquiry in 1939 was my recognition of the importance of the series known as the Swarthmore Lecture, so named because of the home of George Fox. These lectures have become, in our century, the nearest thing we have to an accepted account of Quaker belief in the modern world. The lecturer who understands this will take his or her assignment with great seriousness. The text of 1939 was originally published by the British firm, Allen and Unwin, but now appears, with my full cooperation, as an offering of Friends United Press.

D. Elton Trueblood

Earlham
Spring, 1987

CONTENTS

> " We shall never have a constructive philosophy
> unless we take religious experience seriously."
>
> W. R. MATTHEWS.

THE TRUSTWORTHINESS OF RELIGIOUS EXPERIENCE

I

THE CLAIM TO KNOWLEDGE

It has been one of the distinctive features of Evangelical Religion to emphasize what is called Assurance of Faith, an experimental temper which borders so closely on spiritual certainty, that the believer comes to talk like a Gnostic, and faith appears to mark out for itself a claim in the very area of knowledge.—J. RENDEL HARRIS.

THE present sickness of civilization, of which we are so acutely conscious, is marked by many disturbing symptoms, but none is more disturbing than the present condition of religious faith. Our time cannot be accurately described as a time of irreligion, but rather as one in which we see the alarming growth of what we are forced to recognize as false religions. The most conspicuous of these involve fanatical devotion to living men, whose unworthiness is obvious to any detached observer. It is an elementary, though often neglected, observation on the history of religions, that religion may be extremely harmful as well as beneficial, both to its adherents and to the human race generally. There are bad religions, especially those based on falsehood, and we are deluged with them now.

For a number of reasons the basic faiths, which have done so much to provide a cultural unity to the western world for centuries, have been undermined, and countless people, thus unsettled, have become easy marks for the propagation of new faiths. It has been demonstrated, once more, that the house which is swept and garnished cannot long remain empty.

The closest historical parallel is to be found in the break-up of the antique civilization, when men, having ceased to believe in the objective reality of the pagan gods and goddesses, and having experienced what has been termed a " loss of nerve ", were adopting new faiths. Then, as now, they turned, on the one hand, to emperor worship, with its attendant persecutions, and, on the other hand, to pseudo-mysticism, with its interest in self-culture.

Into the antique civilization there came a message of life and power teaching men to think of the one true God as objectively real, far above all particular men and particular nations, and declaring that men had been granted, and were still granted, direct knowledge of the divine nature. This message turned confusion into order, becoming the central element in a unifying pattern of existence.

It is now abundantly clear to thoughtful persons that the sickness of our civilization requires the vigorous reintroduction of some such central faith. A thorough-going faith in God who is at once universal in sovereignty, spiritual in nature, and Christlike in character, would make the bizarre and sectional religions of our day impossible. Such a faith would give men incentive without hatred and confidence without bombast. It would provide an effective antidote for inflated nationalism and, at the same time, lead men and women to take seriously their responsibilities to their fellow-men, inasmuch as all are children of the same Father. Since the predicament of paganism can hardly fail to be increasingly acute, there is excellent reason to suppose that nothing short of a general return to the Christian faith can counterbalance the disruptive and centrifugal forces of modern life. In the strategy of world salvation it is wise to concentrate on a few points of really vital significance, with the hope that such emphasis may bring conviction to doubters. Thus even the philosopher of religion may have some part in practical regeneration.

When we seek, in a crucial time, to stress what is at once most vital and most persuasive in the Christian religion, we turn quite naturally to the fact of religious experience. Here, if anywhere, we shall find something which appeals to an age which prides itself on being empirically minded. Our people will not listen, for the most part, to discursive arguments, no matter how carefully formulated, but many of them might reasonably be expected to listen to the record of experience. Indeed the willingness to listen to such reports might well be considered a measure of the degree to which the scientific mentality has permeated our society. Whatever else we mean by science, we mean the habit of examining the data rather than the habit of arriving at conclusions on the basis of *a priori* considerations.

The primary datum of religion may be stated as follows : *Millions of men and women, throughout several thousand years, representing various races and nations, and including all levels of education or cultural opportunity, have reported an experience of God as the spiritual companion of their souls.* In prayer and worship, whether at stated times or in the midst of everyday duties, they have been acutely conscious of Another who has sustained them in life's darkest as well as life's brightest moments.

Here, in this record of experience, is one of the major facts of the world. A report so stupendous in scope demands reverent attention as well as analysis. We must face it in the scientific temper of one who is willing to " sit down before fact as a little child ". Conceivably, a careful examination of the available evidence may convince us that the experience is illusory, but by no stretch of the imagination can it be considered unimportant.

Though this experience is as wide as the world, it is only in the Hebrew-Christian tradition that it has been generally used as evidence for God's reality. The tradition to which we belong is replete with expressions of direct contact :

I had heard of thee by the hearing of the ear. but now mine eye seeth thee.

O taste and see that the Lord is good.

Thou wouldst not seek me if thou hadst not already found me.

Statements of this nature are legion. The experience claimed is almost the antithesis of inferential knowledge and has little to do with speculation. How different this is from characteristic Greek thought ! We are, indeed, in another world when we read Xenophon's teleological argument or even the famous Tenth book of Plato's *Laws*. Plato uses three arguments, that from the consensus of the opinions of mankind, that from the idea of Soul as an original causal factor, and that from the order of nature, but he seems not to be aware of an argument from immediate experience. For early Christians, on the other hand, faith in God was a matter of acquaintance rather than speculation. The familiar opening of one of the earliest interpretations of the faith was : " That which was from the beginning, which we have heard, which we have seen with our eyes, and our hands have handled." In a similar strain St. Paul could say, " I *know* in whom I have believed." We must remember that it was a religion with this vigorous and forthright appeal that entered the Roman world with such power.

It is instructive to note the way in which the appeal to direct experience is related to the classical arguments for the existence of God. While it is a mistake to say, as some do, that the metaphysical proofs, especially the ontological, cosmological and teleological, are worthless,* it is accurate to say that alone they are strikingly insufficient. They give us presumptive evidence for something, but not for the God whom we love and worship. If, however, God be known in experience, the metaphysical proofs are valuable as intellectual buttresses to our faith. " Experience " needs " proofs " to establish plausibility, but the " proofs " need " experience " to make the relation to the Object a religious one. In gaining an understanding of this important point many of us have listened with profit to Professor C. C. J. Webb, who writes :

> I do not consider that, apart from the sense, . . . of being in the presence of Something at once *ultimate* and *intimate*, the arguments for the existence of God which may be called metaphysical and which received such drastic treatment at the hands of Kant, could establish the reality of a God who would be the object of religious worship.†

The chief weakness of the traditional proofs lies in the fact that the God to whom they point is an *inference* and it is not as an inference that God has been or can be worshipped. Moreover, with changing metaphysical concepts, one or another of the proofs seems always to be under fire, the one most under fire in contemporary philosophy being the Cosmological Argument.

---

* How brilliantly the ancient arguments can be reconstructed is seen in *The Purpose of God*, by W. R. Matthews.

† C. C. J. Webb, *Religion and Theism*, George Allen & Unwin Ltd., 1934, p. 111. For a similar judgement see William James, *The Varieties of Religious Experience*, p. 437.

We need to remember that a loss of confidence in the Cosmological Argument need not be a calamity for living religion. Religion does not stand or fall by reasonings about a First Cause, but rather by the vindication of belief in God as a present reality, the Divine Companion. A recognition of this is leading to a different emphasis in the philosophy of religion. So considerable a philosopher as Professor A. E. Taylor, of the University of Edinburgh, makes the empirical argument the final one in an ascending series, the first two referring to nature and morality.*

Though the use of the argument from experience is now great, it is by no means universal. Roman Catholic theologians apparently consider the argument dangerous, but it is worth noting that these same theologians consistently interpret other arguments in the light of Christian experience and, by this means, save these arguments from mere formalism. The argument from experience has been rejected by at least one prominent Protestant thinker, Dr. Hastings Rashdall.† It should also be said that some quasi-Barthians have reacted against the emphasis on religious experience, maintaining that such

* A. E. Taylor, "The Vindication of Religion", in *Essays Catholic and Critical*, edited by E. G. Selwyn, Macmillan.

† Hastings Rashdall, *Ideas and Ideals*, Oxford, 1928, Ch. I. Dr. Rashdall's chief contention was that religious experience does not have the same indubitable quality found in intuition, especially mathematical intuition. This may be granted without harm to the present argument, which rests on the same basis as does the argument for dependability in sense experience.

emphasis involves a "subjectivist theology". The chief purpose of this lecture is to show that dependence upon religious experience, far from being subjectivist, cannot be rationally interpreted except in an objective sense.

As we analyse the primary datum of religion, attempting to see precisely what is claimed, especially in the Hebrew-Christian tradition, we find that the claim is twofold :

(1) The experience is claimed, by the believer, to be one of *immediate acquaintance*. That is, it corresponds to what William James called " acquaintance with " rather than " knowledge about ".

(2) The experience is claimed, by the believer, to involve objective reference. That is, it implies a basic realism.

There is no more important question than the question of the truth value of this two-fold claim. We are forced to ask, in the words of William James, " Can philosophy stamp a warrant of veracity on the religious man's sense of the divine ? "*

Though recent theological literature includes a number of excellent studies on this question,†

* William James, *The Varieties of Religious Experience*, p. 430.

† Important titles are *Is Christian Experience an Illusion ?* by Henry Balmforth ; *The Dilemma of Religious Knowledge*, by C. A. Bennett ; *Religious Experience, its Nature, Types and Validity*, by A. C. Bouquet ; *The Validity of Religious Experience*, by F. E. England ; *The Validity of Religious Experience*, by A. C. Knudson ; and *The Logic of Religious Thought*, by R. G. Milburn.

there is still room for another approach to it, especially one from the standpoint of Quaker experience. There is a considerable body of Quaker thought which bears on the problem, some of it dating from almost the beginning of the Society of Friends in the Seventeenth Century. Robert Barclay, acknowledged as the greatest of Quaker thinkers, began his famous *Apology* with a strong emphasis on experimental knowledge, his first two propositions dealing with the " Foundation of Knowledge ", and " Immediate Revelation ". " Inward, immediate, objective revelation by the Spirit ", wrote Barclay, " is that, which all professors of Christianity of whatever kind, are forced ultimately to recur unto, when pressed to the last."

Since the question at issue has been much before Friends in recent times, it is not unreasonable to suppose that Friends have a positive contribution to make to its answer. One of the best brief considerations of the subject in modern Quaker literature is to be found in Chapter IX of the Swarthmore Lecture of 1924, which was given by Gerald K. Hibbert. Far more important, however, than the philosophical considerations of the subject in Quaker literature, is the great body of first hand material which Friends have inherited, in the numerous Journals of Friends.

Friends have not, as a people, read much theology in the last two hundred and eighty years, but they have read persistently the records of the inner life of numerous devout souls. Perhaps the most enduring contribution of contemporary Quakerism to religion in general, consists in the fact that it has produced a new type of declaration of faith, that declaration being, in effect, an anthology of religious experience, rather than a credal system.

It may be said by some that it is a waste of effort to deal in a critical manner with religious experience, since those who have it need no convincing, and those who have it not cannot be convinced in any case. Thus argument would be either unnecessary or futile. The true situation seems to be, however, that there are many who are in grave doubt, ready to be convinced. Discussion should help especially three classes of persons :

    (*a*) Those who have had fleeting intimations of divine fellowship, yet doubt the evidence of their minds because of the fear of self delusion.

    (*b*) Those who have been barred from the experimental knowledge of God by a system of belief which renders them insensitive to spiritual things, just as a theory of race might blind them to the beauties of Negro art. Intellectual considerations may be privative.

    (*c*) Those who have had genuine knowledge of God, but have not recognized it as such. This class is probably very numerous.

In order to clarify the issue it is useful to consider the relationship of " religious knowledge " to " religious experience ". The latter term has become, in this century, a " blessed word", much used in popular discussion. Frequently it is implied that experience is self-validating. It ought to be obvious, however, that experience may include almost anything under the sun, falsehood as well as truth.

It seems a pity that the word " *Gnostic* " has come into disrepute by becoming associated with one particular sect in early Christian history.* There is an important sense in which every evangelical Christian may be a Gnostic in that he claims to have genuine knowledge, though he does not claim to have an answer to every conceivable problem. The true Gnostic is perplexed about many things, and perhaps continues to be perplexed to the very end, but there is a single clue that he cannot doubt.

The founders of our faith, though humble, were not for that reason tentative and hypothetical. They were convinced that, in the characteristic experiences of religion, they had come to have real knowledge of God's nature, and were not merely exploring their own minds or idealizing a convenient fiction. This helped greatly to distinguish Christianity from the various forms of pseudo-mysticism which set such store by inner states of consciousness or unconsciousness.

Members of the Society of Friends are

* By the " Gnostics " we mean those belonging to a strong movement, in the first two centuries of our era, which asserted a superior knowledge of spiritual things. The movement was mystical in an esoteric manner.

particularly prone to engage in rather facile talk about the inner life which may easily cover vagueness of thought. It is easy to talk about God being within our souls in such a way as to suggest that God has no independent existence. This tends to confuse God with our idea of God, reducing God to the level of our finite experience. The present Dean of St. Paul's Cathedral has seen this danger so clearly that he refuses to talk about " the Beyond that is within ",* and speaks instead of " the Beyond that is akin ".

Experience may be purely subjective as in the case of the person suffering from *delirium tremens*, who assuredly " sees " certain animals, or it may involve objective reference as in the case of the person who visits the animals in the zoological gardens. Experience is a covering term which includes all kinds of mental states, emotions, aspirations, or what not. Knowledge is a particular kind of experience which, in the nature of the case, involves two terms, a subject and an object. Knowledge is the bridge which crosses the chasm which separates subject from object. We employ, in this part of the discussion, the word " knowledge ", because experience may mean anything, whereas alleged knowledge always claims the quality of veracity. If knowledge is veracious the subject does have some real contact with the object. We have real knowledge when the chasm which separates the knower and the

* The currency of this expression arises from its use as the title of a book by Emile Boutroux.

known is somehow bridged so that we have veridical information about that which is the object of knowing. The Christian religion holds that, in the experience of prayer and worship, the conditions of knowledge are met so that the Christian claim is a knowledge claim.

Such a realistic theory of religious knowledge is strictly parallel to philosophical realism in regard to the several aspects of the external world and it can be defended in a similar manner. The heart of such realism is the conviction that the objects of knowledge, though understood by the knower in the light of his limitations, nevertheless enjoy independent existence. When we say " God exists ", we mean, in the words of Professor C. A. Bennett, that

> In addition to all finite selves there is a being called God, numerically distinct from them, an independent centre of consciousness, with his own unique life and purposes, with a differential activity of his own.*

It is this realistic theory of religious knowledge that is at stake to-day.† Countless people,

---

* C. A. Bennett, *The Dilemma of Religious Knowledge*, Yale University Press, 1931, p. 50. Among all who have dealt with the non-illusory character of religious knowledge in our time, none, in my opinion, has done better service than did Professor Bennett whose early death was a severe loss to philosophical studies. Admirers of Professor Bennett will be glad to know that there is a considerable body of unpublished material from his pen and that there is a promise of its early publication.

† Whenever the terms " realism " and " realistic " are used in this book they are to be understood in the above sense. Philosophical realism, of whatever sort, is thus in opposition to subjectivist theories of knowledge.

whose minds have been slightly tainted by the reading of popular books on psychology, dismiss the tremendous claim of Christian men in a light manner. It is widely believed that men, when they suppose they have a direct apprehension of God are merely projecting their own wishes, desires, hopes, and ideals on the external order. This form of attack is frequently convincing, precisely because it is often made with a tone of scientific assurance and without argument, as though none were needed.*   This is often coupled with an analysis of abnormal religious experiences as though they were characteristic of religion in general.   In prayer, according to this hypothesis, a man supposes he is lifted by divine communion, but, in reality, he is engaged in private meditation or is being affected by the emotional interchanges in a group to which he belongs.

The issue thus continually raised is one of paramount importance for the Christian faith as well as for other historical religions. If the cognitive claim cannot be upheld it does not seem likely that religion can continue except in a vestigial form. If men, in the hour of prayer, are only communing with themselves and if they discover, with the growth of self-consciousness, that this is the case, as they eventually will, they will cease to go through the motions. Religion will die of disillusionment, for men are not helped by illusions when they are recognized as such. Honest men can hardly keep up the words and

* The psychological attack is considered in Chapter III.

trappings of faith when a realistic belief in God is gone. " It is better to repudiate religion and all its works than to chatter about worshipping or adoring humanity."* Some philosophers have encouraged prayer because of its psychological efficacy, but those who are convinced by their arguments will find that the efficacy has ceased. William James, though he claimed never to have experienced God's presence,† was intelligent enough to realize that a realistic interpretation of religious knowledge was essential to religion. " The conviction that something is genuinely transacted in this consciousness is ", he wrote, " the very core of living religion."‡

Whether something is actually transacted in religious experience is a problem not unlike that faced in all sense experience. That there is an

* Charles A. Bennett, *The Dilemma of Religious Knowledge*, p. 49.

† *The Letters of William James*, Vol. II, p. 214.

‡ William James, *The Varieties of Religious Experience*, p. 466. While James thus saw the central question with great clarity, he cannot be said to have answered it. I do not find the answers in James that I seek and that I am encouraged to expect. I find Professor John Baillie expressing the same disappointment when he says : " We cannot help feeling that it is to this question that James, as representing a true Psychology of Religion, should have devoted the main part of his volume. Whereas, in fact, it is only in appearance that James' psychology faces the question of the truth of religion ; in reality he balks dead as soon as the question is raised, and puts us off with a bald, unargued, and quite unanalysed statement of his own faith."—*The Interpretation of Religion*, p. 138. Because of his radical empiricism, James did not feel as keenly as do many of us, the question of objectivity.

actual transaction is neither obviously true nor obviously false. Those who report religious experience might be mistaken, as they sometimes are when they report sense experience, and they might be telling the truth. Religion, if it is instinctive as some hold, is not, for that reason, true, and not, for that reason, false. We are helped greatly by remembering constantly that we are considering a claim to knowledge and that it must be tested like any other claim. We ought to test the alleged knowledge of God as we would test the alleged knowledge of a stone. In both cases there are subjective factors since we are bound to receive all messages, whatever their external source, by means of our own human faculties, but it is surely a *non sequitur* to make the recognition of subjective factors tantamount to a denial of objective factors.

If religious experience be denied validity on the ground that it is inwardly experienced, and is therefore a matter of projection, it is difficult to see how one can avoid the full sceptical conclusion and deny *any* objective order, inasmuch as all things we claim to know are inwardly experienced. Why is not every scientific concept, every judgement a " projection " of what is in the mind ? If men wish to carry their epistemological scepticism this far, no one is likely to stop them, but they are notoriously unwilling to do so. They always want to make exceptions to their subjectivism, positing at least the existence of other persons with whom to argue the point.

The reasons ordinarily given for rejecting the validity of religious experience prove far too much, perhaps more than those who use such reasons realize. We do well to remember the dictum of John Stuart Mill, who said, in another connection, " Objections which apply equally to all evidence are valid against none."*

Many people seem to suppose there is some absolute test of veracity in ordinary sensory experience, but reflection shows that none exists. I see an object and the question may arise whether this is just a figment of my imagination or is really there. I go over and touch it, providing the object is near at hand, but this does not prove my original contention ; it merely gives one more item of experience which strengthens the conviction because the different experiences are consistent with each other.

Few who have written on this subject have expressed more convincingly than has Gerald K. Hibbert, the truth that our faith in physical objects and our faith in God rest on similar assumptions which cannot be strictly proved :

There are precisely the same reasons for doubting the existence of the pillar-box that I can see down the street as for doubting the existence of God. In both cases vast assumptions have to be made (though we are often unconscious of making them) and in both cases the doubt is simply a doubt whether our own natural faculties are instruments that tell the truth, whether our own apparent experiences may be trusted as real and

* John Stuart Mill, *Theism*, Uniform edition, p. 219.

actual.   There is no knowledge of any kind which we can acquire without making big assumptions to start with.*

We can never prove beyond a shadow of doubt that there is an objective world at all, but the pan-subjectivist is faced with a tremendous miracle.   If all experiences are merely subjective, how does it come about that there is such a remarkable similarity in the accounts of the world on the part of those working separately ? How does it happen that hundreds of men count the same number of limbs on a tree ?   How does it happen that men have come to apply what Professor Lovejoy calls the *category of publicity*, that is, " the notion of a world of objects for common knowledge " ?   The ordinary man in *all* his moods, and the philosopher in all his moods but one, rejects the miracle of coincidence and accounts for agreement by the hypothesis of objectivity.

It is not the least of Professor Lovejoy's contributions to philosophy that he has pointed out, in a convincing manner, the philosophical realism of the natural man.   The epistemological assumptions of the ordinary man

are all manifestations of the primary and most universal faith of man, his inexpugnable realism, his two-fold belief that he is on the one hand in the midst of realities which are not himself nor mere obsequious shadows of himself, a world which transcends the narrow confines

* G. K. Hibbert, *The Inner Light and Modern Thought*, London, George Allen & Unwin Ltd., 1924, p. 64.

of his own transient being ; and, on the other hand, that he can himself somehow reach beyond those confines and bring those external existences within the compass of his own life, yet without annulment of their transcendence.*

If it can be shown that we have the same reasons for believing in objective reference in religious experience as we have in sense experience it is surely an untenable position to deny the one while accepting the other. Once we have realized clearly that all realism rests on faith, but a faith that is in many ways inevitable, we should be able to consider without prejudice the evidence which drives us to a realistic interpretation of religious knowledge.

The objection might be raised that the comparison of religious experience to sense experience is an unfair one, since the objects of reference are so different. It is one thing to know tangible objects, but it is quite another for a living creature on the earth really to *know* the creating and sustaining Mind of the universe. In answer it can be truly said that all knowledge is so amazing that one claim is no more presumptuous than another. We commonly miss the wonder of knowledge, because we make the claim habitually and confidently, but in truth the wonder of it is very great. We assert that we can take cognizance, not only of what is outside the confines of our bodies, sometimes far distant in space, but also

* A. O. Lovejoy, *The Revolt Against Dualism*, George Allen & Unwin Ltd., 1930, p. 11.

that we can have knowledge of what now is not, inasmuch as it has ceased to be.

As we think about the problem we come to see that alleged knowledge of God is really not more, but rather less amazing than a knowledge of sticks and stones, which are so alien to our natures. This has been well expressed by Rufus M. Jones as follows :

If God is Spirit and man is spirit it is not strange, absurd or improbable that there should be communion and correspondence between them. The odd thing is that we have correspondence with a world of matter, not that we have correspondence with a world of spiritual reality like our own inner nature. The thing that needs explanation is how we have commerce with rocks and hills and sky. It seems natural that we should have commerce with That which is most like ourselves.*

We conclude that there is no justification, either for the person who rejects the testimony of religious experience in advance, on the basis of *a priori* considerations, nor for the one who attributes to his religious experience an infalli- bility which places it beyond criticism. The path of wisdom lies in the subjection of empirical data, of whatever kind, to the best tests of veracity which the human mind has been able to devise.

In a magnificent figure of speech Charles A. Bennett says that the vision of God, the original datum about which we are concerned in this lecture, is not in the form of pure metal, but *ore.* It calls, indeed, for refinement, but there is

* Rufus M. Jones, *The New Quest*, New York, 1928, p. 146.

something to refine. The task of reason is the humble one of the refiner, not the bold one of the prospector. " Reason may establish our certainties ; it does not initiate them."*

* Charles A. Bennett, *A Philosophical Study of Mysticism,* p. 110.

II

The Test of Knowledge

On all questions about religion there is the most distressing divergency. But the saints do not contradict one another. They all tell the same story. They claim to have had glimpses of the land that is very far off, and they prove that they have been there by bringing back perfectly consistent and harmonious reports of it.—Dean Inge.

The fundamental test of objectivity is the test of agreement, and indeed there is no other. If the objects seen by the patient suffering from delirium were seen in equal measure by other men, particularly by men not suffering from *disease*, including a significant proportion of men in whom the critical spirit reigns, and if this convergence of testimony should last over long periods of time, we should be forced to hold, by the only criteria available to us, that these " objects " do have some kind of real existence independent of the thought of the delirious person.

The agreement which constitutes the criterion of objectivity takes several forms, depending upon the precise nature of the experience in question. In sense experience the agreement we expect is threefold :

(a) Agreement of the report with what is reported by other means at the individual's command, particularly other senses. Thus we frequently check sight with touch.

(b) Agreement of the report with what is reported by other observers, particularly those in varying conditions. Thus astronomers are continually checking each other's observations. It is desirable to have a large number of such reporters, providing they are qualified.

(c) Agreement with the general world view to which we have been led by experience of various kinds. Any new claim is suspect if it contradicts what is generally known as true. Sometimes, however, we are forced to accept the new claim and make the consequent alteration in our world view.

In religious experience the types of agreement we should consider sufficient to establish the warrantable assertability of objective reference are slightly different, since we have nothing in this area to compare with the plurality of the senses. The experience of God is not a matter of separate organs, but an experience of the whole person in response to the divine. Accordingly we must eliminate the first of the three tests given above, as we should do in considering the experience of beauty, but this leaves us the second and third. The third is the province of the metaphysical proofs of God's reality, to which we have already alluded, and which are discussed admirably in many books. What these proofs attempt to do is to show that God's being is consistent with or demanded by, a great variety of phenomena, especially those having to do with the order of nature and the appearance of moral values.

We are left, then, with the second of our three types of agreement, perhaps the one which is most significant of all and certainly the most convincing. In order to be convincing, however, it is necessary to show three things : first, that the reporters of religious experience are numerous ; second, that a sufficient number of them are creditable and trustworthy persons ; and, third, that their reports are mutually consistent.

There seems to be a widespread conviction to-day that those who have an experience of God are so few as to be negligible. If that were true their testimony might conceivably be dismissed, but even so it would hardly be taken lightly by intelligent men who realized at all fully the exciting nature of the testimony. Probably the chief reason for the notion that religious experience is rare is that many have thought of such experience as being something connected with trance or heavenly visions or even " speaking with tongues ". It must be admitted that some of the writers on mysticism have been partly responsible for the spread of such conceptions, because of the types they have studied. Even William James, who wrote what continues to be a major work in the Psychology of Religion, dealt almost wholly with what can only be called queer cases.

There *are* queer cases of religious experience, but it is absurd to consider them typical or normal. Where there has been one who has heard voices there have been thousands whose religious experience has included nothing of the kind, but has, instead, been nothing more fantastic than an awareness of the sustaining love of God, the Divine Companion. For most, this has not been connected with dreams of any kind, but has been part and parcel of their normal, waking hours. Religion is not a branch of abnormal psychology.

We are fortunate in having, in the experience of John Wilhelm Rowntree, a beautiful illustration which shows how normal and wholesome the sense of the divine presence can be. The words of Rufus Jones about his friend cannot but live :

Just as he was entering young manhood and was beginning to feel the dawning sense of a great mission before him, he discovered that he was slowly losing his sight and hearing. He was told that before middle life he would become totally blind. Dazed and overwhelmed he staggered from the doctor's office into the street and stood there in silence. Suddenly he felt the love of God wrap him about as though a visible presence enfolded him, and a joy filled him, such as he had never known before. From that time until this joy was deepened into the new life of to-day, he was a gloriously joyous and happy man.*

* *The American Friend*, March 16th, 1905. This was written soon after the untimely death of John Wilhelm Rowntree.

The experiences of trance may be religious experiences, but they are not characteristic ones and the case for realism would be quite as good if these reports of the unusual were not part of the record. By spiritual experience we mean nothing more strange or bizarre than that which comes to a humble worshipper in prayer, whether the prayer be public or private. The person to whom prayer is meaningful, and not merely a dull routine exercise, is conscious that there are two parties in the undertaking. Without a personal certainty that there were two parties, prayer would hardly continue from generation to generation. Furthermore, such experience is not limited to moments of prayer, but is often a steady assurance as the background of work in the world. Frequently this sense of assurance or " backing " is greatest in moral decisions. It should be clear, therefore, that when we speak of religious experience we do not refer to what is rare, but rather to what has been felt by great numbers, perhaps even a majority of men, in the last few thousand years.

Another misunderstanding that must be avoided is that which practically equates religion and philosophy, so that the word God stands for an explanatory concept. This would, indeed, make religion rare, but genuine religion would be neglected. " The heart of Religion ", as has been well said by the present Archbishop of York, " is not an opinion about God, such as Philosophy might reach as the conclusion of its argument ;

it is a personal relationship with God."* When we think of God as the Companion of prayer and not a term in an argument, we begin to realize how widespread religious experience really is. It may be reported with gratitude that, in current philosophical discussion, there seems to be an increasing tendency to use the word " God " to refer to what the plain man means by it. The late Lord Balfour, especially in his Gifford Lectures, contributed influentially to this tendency. What he said then is equally applicable in this connection:

> When I speak of God I mean something other than an Identity wherein all differences vanish, or a Unity which includes but does not transcend the differences which it somehow holds in solution. I mean a God whom men can love, a God to whom men can pray, who takes sides, who has purposes and preferences, whose attributes, howsoever conceived, leave unimpaired the possibility of a personal relationship between Himself and those whom He has created.†

By the most conservative estimate the number of persons who have reported religious experience, not in the sense of ecstatic trance, and not in the sense of a merely rational inference, but as a deep assurance of the divine under-girding, is many millions and, indeed, it is difficult to think of any similar data that are so numerous. The early writings of the Hebrew people, with which we are

* William Temple, *Nature, Man and God*, London, 1934, p. 54.

† A. J. Balfour, *Theism and Humanism*, New York, 1915, p. 36. For a similar forthrightness, see Professor W. P. Montague, *Belief Unbound*, Yale University Press, 1930, pp. 6, 7.

familiar in our Old Testament, abound with
expressions of faith based on direct experience.
Frequently, of course, the reports used the
language of sense, but we should not be bothered
by figures of speech. The point is that men
claimed they had known God, and found that it
was good to know Him. The Psalms as well as
the speeches of the Hebrew prophets abound with
reports that God has been known as a saving
power.

In the New Testament we find a similar
abundance of reports, the high point being the
experience of Christ. Even with the interval of
the years and the changes in language the simple
immediacy and reality are obvious in the prayers
of Jesus, " I thank Thee, O Father, Lord of
Heaven and Earth." One who makes such a
prayer is convinced that he is in direct contact
with the Answerer of prayer. It is not a speech
to the crowd and not a private meditation. *Part
of our datum is the fact that the one who has most
won the loyalty of men, himself experienced the
companionship and sustaining power of God.*

And thus it has gone on through the succeeding
centuries, the data occurring among the highest
as well as the lowest among men. Though we
are confining our data chiefly to the Christian
tradition it may be pointed out that experience
of God is normal and general in all religions, even
Buddhism, which at first was not definitely
theistic, finally coming into line, at least so far
as the popular faith is concerned.

It is interesting to note that the religious literature which has been best loved through many generations has been that which reports experience and thus adds to the available data. The *Confessions* of St. Augustine gain much of their appeal from this first hand quality.

Though only the gifted few have been able to write of their religious experience, this does not mean that it is limited to such. The millions who have known what it is to pray or to be conscious, in worship, of the " real Presence ", add to the stupendous fact. Many who would never think of writing down what they have experienced are able to tell it to their fellows as they have long done in the testimony meetings which stem from the Wesleyan revival. If we attend such an " experience meeting " and refuse to be bothered by the stereotyped expressions, we often get an overwhelming sense of the weight of the report. The testimony meeting corresponds to the gathering of data in a scientific enterprise. One after another, in perfect sincerity, arises to say, " Once I was blind, but now I see." " I sought the Lord and he heard me." " I know that my Redeemer liveth." Sometimes the sentences are not so felicitous, but what the simple believer is saying is, " I prayed to God and I came to know Him as a regenerating power. Now I walk with a new step." Not many can say with George Fox, " Now was I come up through the flaming sword into the Paradise of God ", but they clearly mean much the same. These common people,

just as the learned ones like St. Augustine, have
known a Power not themselves, and this knowledge has changed the course of their lives.   They
have known a response to their cries and it has
made a difference.   It is possible that they are all
deluded, but it is important that we know how
many men and what sort of men we are accusing
when we say this.

It seems probable that most of those who
undertake so lightly to relegate religious experience to the limbo of subjectivism have not fully
appreciated how enormous their undertaking
really is.

When we have realized, with some fullness,
the large body of evidence with which we have to
deal in considering whether all religious experience
is illusory, we have also made a good start towards
the answer to our second question, that regarding
the character of the reporters.   It is fantastic
to suppose that, when so many are concerned,
all reporters are untruthful or biased in some
manner by constitutional difficulties.   If there
could be shown a one-to-one correspondence
between some kind of emotional instability and
the claim to a trans-subjective knowledge of
God, we should rightly suspect the evidence, but
no one seriously holds that such correspondence
can be demonstrated.   When we realize that our
enormous company includes not only ascetic
persons like Bernard of Clairvaux, but men of
learning like Boyle and Newton, and men of the
world like William Penn, as well as countless

humble people of all types, we see how unsupported is the hypothesis that religious experience is the result of a diseased mind. Certainly the evidence shows no particular connection with marriage or lack of marriage, and is not confined to either sex. Canon Raven has stated the case for religious sanity in a manner worth repeating here :

> The simple fact is, of course, that those who would explain away religion are hardly aware of the greatness of the task or of the qualifications necessary for it. To indict the supreme representatives of mankind from the Buddha to Plato and from Jeremiah to Jesus as paranoiacs is to challenge man's whole ability to appreciate value. If these be mad, who is sane ? If these be mad then madness is more beautiful, more reasonable, more beneficent, more effective than sanity.*

It may be said in passing that the above considerations, while true, need not blind us to the genuine importance of some who seem unbalanced, often because they are more sensitive than their fellows. Those who are very frail physically sometimes have an especially keen insight because of their very detachment from the little interests of normal healthy living. We should not despise what men learn on beds of pain. " Nature ", as Dean Inge reminds us, " often gives with one hand what she takes away with the other."† Poets are often eccentric, but we do not, for that reason, discount or reject their *poetic* insight.

* Charles E. Raven, *Jesus and the Gospel of Love*, Hodder & Stoughton, London, 1931, p. 73.

† W. R. Inge, *Studies of English Mystics*, p. 25.

For the purpose of our present argument we are at pains to show that most of those who testify to an immediate acquaintance with God as Divine Companion are perfectly normal people, engaged in ordinary, wholesome tasks, and fortunately free from physical or mental defects. It is quite possible, however, that the *highest* types of religious experience have come to those who have suffered in some unfortunate way.*

The third question, that concerning the actual agreement of reports, is the crucial one. Even though those who have religious experience are wonderfully numerous and though the reporters are men of character and sanity, there is still reason for valid doubt that such experience produces knowledge, in the realistic sense, if the reports themselves are a hopeless jumble. Superficially they do often seem to be such a jumble. All observers are aware of the fact that there are many religions and many warring sects within particular religions. The apparent diversity of the reports, especially about the nature of God, has led some serious thinkers to argue for subjectivity at this point. Thus Durant Drake :

We know that a seen object is an objective reality because we can also touch or hear or smell it, or in some way check up our optical sensations ; otherwise we suspect them to be mere hallucinations or mal-observations. So with the data offered by a " religious sense " ;

* This explains why it is that books on mysticism so often seem like books on abnormal psychology.

they must be corroborated by the rest of our experience. And since we find, as a matter of fact, that the "religious" sense of one man perceives one kind of a God, and that of another a radically different God, we not unnaturally suspect that this " sense " is a merely supposed source and explanation of those deep-rooted beliefs that in most men's minds antedate and outlive argument and evidence.*

This is a serious objection and we may as well admit, at the outset, that much religious experience will not meet the test of agreement. Some is obviously illusory inasmuch as some of the reports are strictly contradictory. It cannot be possible, for instance, that God has a body and that God does not have a body, providing we are careful in our use of terms and precise in our meanings. All kinds of strange claims have been made by people under emotional strain. Let us remind ourselves, however, that contradictions and bizarre reports occur in *every* kind of experience ; in other fields, we do not immediately jump to the conclusion that there is no objective factor. The history of science is full of conflicting reports about the physical order, many of which are almost certainly false, but we do not therefore conclude that all physical scientists are dealing with nothing but their own subjective states. Objective existence does not necessitate *complete* agreement in reports any more than it necessitates *complete* universality in awareness of it. There are excellent reasons why some reporters are far less able and trustworthy than others. What

* Durant Drake, *Problems of Religion*, pp. 329, 330.

counts in natural science is not entire agreement of all observers, which probably never occurs, but, what is far more important, the substantial agreement of *qualified* observers, especially over a fairly long period of time, and under varying conditions.

Moreover, it is important to watch for *increasing* agreement. We find savage peoples differing, in an extreme fashion, about the constitution of the earth, the heavenly bodies and the size of these objects. But with the growth of critical intelligence all peoples have progressively less differences about these matters until civilized persons have almost none. A recognition of this fact shows how unfair and unreasonable it is to try to discredit the realistic interpretation of religious experience by stressing the differences between primitive faiths. Such an argument, if taken seriously, proves far too much. It is a respectable metaphysical principle that the true nature of anything is better seen in its most perfected form. What we must watch for, then, is not complete agreement, but *substantial* and *progressive* agreement. A good example of progressive agreement is found in the tendency, with advancing culture in many independent settings, to experience God as *one* rather than *many*.

That there is substantial agreement is the sober conclusion of many serious students of the evidence. Among those who have called attention to the fundamental agreement in the experience to which religious men in all ages bear witness are Dean Inge, Dr. Rendel Harris, Professor William James, and Sainte-Beuve. The conclusion reached by Dean Inge appears at the head of this chapter and that of Dr. Harris is familiar to the readers of his matchless devotional books.*

It is interesting to observe that both William James, in his study of many experiences, and Sainte-Beuve, in his intensive study of one movement, came to the conclusion that there is a common element and that it consists in saintliness rather than doctrine. Their sober judgements are as follows :

There is a certain composite photograph of universal saintliness, the same in all religions, of which the features can easily be traced.†

Penetrate a little beneath the diversity of circumstances, and it becomes evident that in Christians of different epochs it is always one and the same modification by which they are affected : there is veritably a single fundamental and identical spirit of piety and charity, common to those who have received grace ; an inner state which before all things is one of love and humility, of infinite confidence in God, and of severity for one's self, accompanied with tenderness for others.‡

The evidence for the truth of these conclusions on the part of those who have probed beneath

---

* He quotes, in one place, a Moslem prayer, points out its similarity to " Lead, Kindly Light ", and says, " I can imagine that it could be used, with very slight reserve, in St. Paul's Cathedral." *The Guiding Hand of God*, p. 20.

† William James, *The Varieties of Religious Experience*, p. 271.

‡ Sainte-Beuve, *Port Royal*, Vol. I, p. 106.

superficial differences begins to appear when we
contrast the record of religion with the record of
science over a period of several thousand years.
The science of a thousand years ago seems ludicrous
and even that of a century ago seems quaint, but
men who report religious experience can speak to
one another across chasms of time without
difficulty.   The religious experience recorded by
the author of the Book of Job in dialogue and by
John Greenleaf Whittier in verse is essentially
the same experience.   If it be suggested that this
is because Whittier learned from the ancient
sage, we can point to a like similarity where
borrowing is out of the question.   On the hypothesis of subjectivity this coincidence is a sheer
miracle.   How little time and place count has
been well shown by the former Dean of St. Paul's :

We need not trouble ourselves to ask, and we could
seldom guess without asking, whether a paragraph
describing the highest spiritual experiences was written
in the Middle Ages or in modern times, in the north or
south of Europe, by a Catholic or by a Protestant.*

To test Dean Inge's assertion let us take one
such report and ask ourselves whether we could
date it :

And He hath many times refreshed my soul in his
presence, and given me assurance that I knew that estate
in which He will never leave me, nor suffer me to be
drawn from all which He has graciously fulfilled ; for
though various infirmities and temptations beset me, yet

* W. R. Inge, *Studies of English Mystics*, p. 35.

my heart cleaveth unto the Lord, in the everlasting bonds that can never be broken.*

We can, however, go farther than Dean Inge's challenge and show that when all are translated into the same language the Christian and non-Christian testimonies have a solid basis of agreement. This does not mean that one religion is as good as another or that Christians are not the heirs of a unique revelation. Many of the features of Christian experience are unique, but the presence of unique factors does not entail the absence of common factors. Since we are concerned, in this book, with the construction of an answer to those who deny *any* objective reference in religious experience, our case is strengthened by pointing to common elements which have the same evidential value as do common elements in sense experience. Though, in sense experience, some observers have unique advantages, the case for basic realism is made, not by pointing to these, but rather by pointing to agreements among those widely separated.

* The above paragraph is taken from an autobiographical fragment, written by Mary Penington before 1668, which constitutes one of the clearest and most convincing records of spiritual life in existence. The " account " was left by Mary Penington with her daughter, the wife of William Penn, but it was not printed until more than a century after her death, 1797. Several printings have been made since, the most convenient being that edited by Norman Penney and published in Philadelphia and London in 1911, with the title, *Experiences in the Life of Mary Penington* (written by herself). Most of the account has the dateless quality of the quotation given above.

It is a matter for regret that it has become theologically fashionable in our time to revive the notion that all other religions are man's own work, if not the Devil's, whereas Christianity alone is God's work: We should need to be wise, indeed, in order to be certain that God has not made Himself directly known to any outside the Christian tradition. A colourless deism is not the only alternative to our fashionable Neo-Fundamentalism. It is thoroughly possible, as the Preface to the Epistle to the Hebrews suggests, that God should reveal Himself partially to many and fully to a few. The really amazing fact is the sense of familiarity we experience when we read supposedly alien testimonies.*

When we are faced with a number of religious testimonies it is often genuinely difficult to determine the theological setting of each without reference to notes. Consider, for example, the following reports :

The man who has beheld God
As his own self face to face ;
The Lord of that which was and is to be,
He feels no fear, nor hides himself in dread.
He who beholds the Loftiest and Deepest,
For him the fetters of the heart break asunder,
For him all doubts are resolved,
And all his works become nothingness.

* The incredulous will be convinced by reading the translations of Indian lyrics which Mahatma Gandhi made in jail. He put these into rough English prose and John S. Hoyland supplied the verse form. The book is called *Songs from Prison*, George Allen & Unwin Ltd., 1934.

All worldly attainments, whether of greatness, wisdom, or bravery, are but empty sounds ; and there is nothing wise or great or noble, but rightly to know and heartily worship and adore the great God that is the support and life of all spirits, whether in Heaven or on earth.

Many hundreds of years separate these two brief testimonies, as well as thousands of miles and profound difference in cultural background, but they breathe the same spirit.   This similarity is close as long as it is testimonies of experience that are concerned, but great variation appears when we consider the inferences which men have drawn on the basis of experience.   Thus the theological formulations are often sufficiently different to provide material for angry dispute, when the original data of the disputants have much in common.   It is easier for men to agree on the Lord's Prayer than on any conceivable creed.   This is not to say that we can avoid the construction of creeds, or that theological argument is fruitless, but it is to say that we miss-fire when we point to theological argument in order to disparage objective reference in religious experience.

It is not surprising to learn that a great part of religious testimony that can be made intelligible soon assumes the quality of song. " Song and poetry ", writes Professor Hocking, " are forms which infinitely repeatable truth must take."*

* William E. Hocking, *The Meaning of God in Human Experience*, Yale University Press, 1928, p. 452.

This is what has happened in the formation of the Hebrew Psalter. Though we seldom give it a thought, it is really a remarkable fact that so many persons, for so many centuries, in spite of advances in civilizations, continue to find in the Psalms the best expression of their own faith. Our western life is different, in all external respects, from that of the nomadic men east of the Mediterranean Sea who first wrote the matchless words which have been sung so long and in so many different languages. Mere tradition will not account for this phenomenon, in view of the fact that we leave off to-day so much that is merely traditional.

We are so familiar with the great Psalms that we often miss their grandeur. This is conspicuously true of one like Psalm 139, which is nothing more nor less than a poetic expression of religious experience.

If I take the wings of the morning, and dwell in the uttermost parts of the sea ;
Even there shall thy hand lead me, and thy right hand shall hold me.

Now the fact that men, generation after generation, give hearty assent to these great words is like the situation in which men agree concerning the number of limbs on the trees. Though most men have not taken the trouble to write reports of their spiritual experience we are not therefore kept totally in the dark concerning the nature of their experiences, inasmuch as their satisfaction in the words of others tells us a great deal. The enduring appeal of the Psalms means that the common man in various generations feels that these songs say what he would like to say also, if only he could.

A similar evidence of fundamental agreement over a long period is found in the widespread use of sermon texts. Some use of texts is purely conventional, but the practice arose spontaneously in the first instance and has been continued by many who are far from conventional. The reason is that ancient words of insight frequently apply in one period quite as well as another, and those who seek to nurture the spiritual life of their fellows find that they can do no better than return to classic expressions.

Recognizing, then, the abundant evidence of agreement we may profitably seek to point, with some precision, to that about which men of various countries are agreed. Among the many common features of the experience three stand out prominently. First, it is agreed that there is in the presence of God an absolute and compelling quality, which, for the time at least, allays doubt, and demands obedience. Men have resorted to a number of figures of speech to express this coercive aspect of the experience, the most common figures being associated with light and fire. Other figures, like those used by Isaiah and Ezekiel, emphasize splendour. The experience is old, indeed, but to each individual it comes as one of compelling novelty. This first important aspect of fundamental agreement is well illustrated in

the records left by two brilliant men of the
seventeenth century, one a Protestant living in
England, and the other a Roman Catholic living
in France. Isaac Penington was able to say, in
a manner calculated to allay all doubt about his
sincerity, " This is He ; this is He ; there is no
other ; this is He whom I have waited for and
sought after from my childhood, who was always
near me, and had often begotten life in my heart,
but I knew him not distinctly, nor how to receive
him, or dwell with him."*

This report of Penington, stressing as it does
the sense of certainty, may profitably be compared
with the account of Pascal's conversion, which
was found in his coat after his death. Penington
and Pascal were contemporaries, though they
lived in very different conditions. Penington's
" convincement " and Pascal's conversion came
in the same decade, that amazing sixth decade
of the seventeenth century which was, in so many
ways, a flowering time of the human spirit in
spite of dark clouds. The beginning of Pascal's
famous document is unforgettable :

> In the year of grace 1654
> Monday the 23rd of November, feast of St. Clement,
> Pope and Martyr, and others of the Martyrology,

---

* These words appear in connection with Thomas Ellwood's
Testimony concerning Isaac Penington, and were dated,
Aylesbury, May 15th, 1667. They apparently refer to an
experience in 1658. This and a large body of interesting
material of a similar nature is found in *The Works of Isaac
Penington*, London, 1681. Penington's testimony is easily
available in *Christian Life, Faith and Thought in the Society
of Friends*, pp. 36-8.

Vigil of St. Chrysogone, martyr, and others, from about half-past ten in the evening to about half-past twelve.

FIRE

" God of Abraham, God of Isaac, God of Jacob,"
Not of philosophers and scholars,
Certainty, Joy, Certainty, Feeling, Light, Joy,
God of Jesus Christ, . . .
Forgetting of the world and of all save God,
He is only to be found in the ways taught in the Gospel.

Here, as in Penington's account, we cannot but be struck by the sense of certainty. Pascal could no more doubt God than he could doubt the fire which warms, lights and even burns. All of the words may be considered as interjections emphasizing the assurance. Certainty comes first in the list of descriptive words and then appears twice.

All over the world and in succeeding generations we find this same certainty. It is logically distinct from the kind of certainty we get in mathematics on the one hand (perhaps a matter of tautology), and from mere probability on the other. This is the type of certainty which we know primarily in relation to persons. I am more certain of the love and loyalty of a few persons than I am of anything else in the world and could far more easily believe in the failure of the earth to rotate on its axis than in the unfaithfulness of these persons. But what is my basis of trust ? By no stretch of the imagination could it fit the requirements of a calculus of probability, but neither does my trust include what is usually called logical *necessity*. Such certainty is an irreducible factor in experience, a factor which enters normally or even habitually into the language of religion.

It is not true to say that there has been complete or even general agreement concerning the personal nature of God, but it is most significant to observe the high degree of agreement concerning the assurance felt by the worshipper which is, as we have shown, the kind which, otherwise, we only find appropriate in connection with persons. The question whether God is personal is a question of theory on which men are divided, but the essentially personal nature of the *relationship to God* is a matter of experience on which they are united.

A second point of agreement lies in the self-depreciation which accompanies the vision of God. One after another the saints, both prominent and obscure, have bowed their heads in shame and admitted, in the light of God's presence, that their own righteousness is filthy rags. This part of the experience, so well known that it needs no illustration, is especially important in that it bears consistent witness to the objective status of the source of the experience. The recognition of personal unworthiness on the part of the worshipper has been, at all times, a vivid admission that he has been the *host*, that the experience did not originate with him. Men have not supposed, for the most part, that they have seen God by virtue of their own goodness, but rather that they have been able to see the bitter truth about themselves by virtue of the recognition of God's presence.

A third aspect of agreement consists in the way in which the sense of unworthiness is followed by creative moral results. Many lives are made new, and frequently the whole direction is changed, as was true of St. Paul after his experience on the road to Damascus. One of the most thrilling aspects of world history is that according to which the consciences of men have been made sensitive by their experiences of God so that they have begun to work for moral and social advances in spite of the lethargy of the masses of men in regard to such questions. This aspect of the agreement is what Professor Hocking calls " the positive contribution of the mystic and the prophet to the concrete spiritual wealth of mankind, a creativity to which we can discern no limit ",* and it is what St. Paul calls " the fruits of the spirit ", the fruits being remarkably similar in all lands.

Religion and morals are by no means identical, but it is a fact of history that their close association has seemed perfectly normal to peoples of the greatest dissimilarity in other ways. The question, " What doth the Lord require of thee ? " is almost a universal question, shown even in the elaborate system of restrictions involved in many primitive faiths. We do not contend that people

* W. E. Hocking, *The Meaning of God in Human Experience*, p. 460.

have been in agreement about what they ought to do, since that has depended, in large measure, on the education of conscience, but we do contend that the religious experience has normally entailed moral demands.

This three-fold agreement really follows a dramatic movement, the classic expression of this movement being found in Isaiah's account of his own vision of God. First, he saw the Lord as a coercive reality ; second, he knew that he was a man of unclean lips ; third, he was able to say, " Here am I, send me." The admission that this record is classic and catholic is an admission of basic agreement.

The value of this evidence lies in its cumulative effect. Agreement about one thing might conceivably be attributed to coincidence or to the similarity of the observers, but as the area of agreement widens with the progress of critical intelligence, the hypothesis of coincidence becomes harder and harder to uphold. The most reasonable explanation of the agreement is that men of all ages are reporting what is true.

III

Removal of Specific Objections

And as our removal of objections to the reality of an external world necessarily establishes its reality for us—because there is the vivid impression, the sense of a trans-human reality all around us, which clamours to be taken as it gives itself, and which was only refused to be thus taken because of those objections ; so now our removal of objections to the reality of the Superhuman Reality necessarily establishes the reality for us—since there, again, is the vivid impression, the sense of a still deeper, a different, trans-human Reality which penetrates and sustains ourselves and all things, and clamours to be taken as It gives Itself.

BARON VON HÜGEL.

THOSE who have followed the argument to this point may be expected to say, " Yes, the case thus presented would be convincing were there not certain special difficulties that are involved in the very nature of religious experience." Because there are particular objections which often hinder a full recognition of the realistic character of religious knowledge, it is necessary at this point to deal with these frankly and with as much care as is possible.

A. Lack of Universality

The first problem arises from the elementary observation that the report of religious experience

is not strictly universal. Religion may be universal
in the sense that there is no people without it,
regardless of their cultural level, but it is not
universal in the sense that all individuals recognize
its claims. We cannot avoid the fact that many
people assert that they do not have, and have
never had, an awareness of God. This is even
true of a considerable number who believe in God
on inferential grounds.

Why, if God is objectively real, as the argument
from experience so far developed would seem to
show, are not all men aware of Him ? Everyone,
we are told, can see the tree on the lawn, everyone
can touch the stone, but not everyone experiences
God's presence.

We are well on the way to an answer to this
question when we realize that all knowing involves
conditions, and the conditions vary with different
objects of knowledge. There are conditions of
sight, which include light, healthy optic nerves,
etc. As a matter of fact, it is not true that all men
see the tree on the lawn, since some men are blind.
Perhaps no type of experience is *strictly* universal.
Sight, however, is practically universal and
presents no particular problem, but we face the
same problem as that found in religious experience
when we leave such easy levels. By no means all
men experience the more profound beauties of art
or music, but we do not ordinarily conclude from
this that those who experience these beauties are
self-deluded. It is the continual lesson of life
that we become progressively aware of more areas,

and we do not seriously expect anything of importance to be obvious to everybody. We should not expect the Presence of God to be known by those who fail to meet the appropriate conditions or who lack the appropriate discipline, any more than we expect such an event in a scientific or aesthetic enterprise. Of course, delusion is always possible and sometimes men, looking through microscopes, see what is not really there, but the fact remains that vision comes only to the prepared. This is particularly true in the use of such an instrument as the ophthalmoscope. A physician, with whom I am intimately acquainted, has told me how he looked long and faithfully into a human eye, without seeing anything ; then suddenly, when he had learned what to look for and his own eyes were fully adjusted to their new task, he saw. Much is now self-evident to him that is by no means self-evident to the ordinary layman. *Truths can be self-evident without being evident to everybody.**

As we reflect more on the subject we are surprised that anyone should present the lack of universality as a serious argument against the validity of religious experience. The only experiences which cost nothing, and are therefore open to all indiscriminately, are the poorest and simplest. What we know is determined, in a

---

* This has been said many times and with such good effect that it is hard to know who first coined the phrase. For a modern example of its use, see Hastings Rashdall, *Ideas and Ideals*, Oxford, 1928, p. 12. The concept is expressed by Richard Hooker in his distinction between certainty and evident certainty. The general notion goes back to Plato.

large degree, by what we are.   That this fact has long been recognized by devout persons is indicated by the continued popularity of the medieval hymn, which includes the lines :

> The love of Jesus, what it is,
> None but his loved ones know.

Few in our time have argued this more persuasively than has Aldous Huxley, especially in words like the following :

Those who have not undertaken the training can have no knowledge of the kind of experiences open to those who have undertaken it and are as little justified in denying the validity of those direct intuitions of an ultimate spiritual reality, at once transcendent and immanent, as were the Pisan professors who denied, on *a priori* grounds, the validity of Galileo's direct intuition (made possible by the telescope) of the fact that Jupiter has several moons.*

It is not surprising that men should doubt the reality of experiences reported by others when they have not had these experiences personally, but it *is* surprising that they should expect these experiences without a careful regard to the necessary conditions.   I cannot reasonably use as negative evidence my failure to see the moons of Jupiter if I never take the trouble to look through a telescope on a clear night.   And yet many people report impressively their lack of experience of God's presence when they have not earned the right to expect that experience. There are certain moods which might well be

* Aldous Huxley, *Ends and Means*, London, 1938, p. 289.

supposed to hinder effectively spiritual communion, conspicuous among these being the moods of the scorner, of the braggart, of the profane, of the supercilious. It is hardly to be expected, even in the hypothesis of God as existent, that the man who jests about Him, will be aware of God's existence *while* he is jesting.

The person who enters into worship with an attitude of " Show me if you can ", will not, in the ordinary course of events, be shown ; he will not even understand what worship is. On the other hand, the most auspicious situation would be one in which the individual would sit down with his fellows or alone, in reverent quietness, aware of his own weakness and ignorance. The eyes of the soul are cleared by silence, by purity of heart, by personal humility, by self discipline. Sometimes we must expect the necessary discipline to be long, as it usually is in the appreciation of great music. Why should it be easier to know God than to understand the fine emotions of a great composer ? Why should we assume the need of careful discipline in order to understand Einstein and not assume an equally rigorous, though different discipline in order to discern the Mind responsible for the principle of which Einstein has had glimpses ? This discipline is a special combination of habitual reverence and consistent effort to do God's will in so far as it has been shown us. It is not merely paradoxical to reverse Mrs. Browning's famous line and to say, " Only he who takes off his shoes, *sees*."

Another part of the answer to the objection that religious experience is not universal lies in pointing to the vast area of experience which is quasi-religious, but not explicitly seen as such. There is in the world a vast amount of what Donald Hankey, in *A Student in Arms*, called "The Religion of the Inarticulate". We can find reverence without ever going into places set aside for worship, just as we sometimes find fundamental irreverence within such places.

It is important to recognize the existence of levels of reverence through which people may be led by steps, as they can be led into an appreciation of poetry by beginning with less advanced forms. The reverence of some is nothing more than a wholesome sense of the mystery of life, some experience wonder in response to natural grandeur, and others experience wonder in response to moral grandeur. The highest level, that of conscious communion with God, is not the only one. Many suppose they do not have religious experience because they have had the wrong expectation. Frequently good people, by making their sense of God seem wonderfully vivid and definite, really do harm, since they lead those who do not have an experience so vivid and definite to suppose they have none at all. On the other hand some devout persons have done a service by admitting that their sense of God's presence has been fleeting and piecemeal. They have glimpses, intimations, hints, but these, if followed, often lead to the certainty of which we have already spoken. Yet even the certainty may be interrupted by times of doubt. Have we ever fully understood the pathos of the cry, " My God, my God, why hast thou forsaken me ? "

Many have found that, by following out the hints of their imperfect faith, the hints grow stronger, just as the eye becomes clearer by the use of the microscope. We must not despise even the slightest appearance of spiritual life, for it may grow.

What shall we say of the person who faithfully puts himself in the condition which facilitates spiritual sight, keeps up the discipline over a long period, and yet reports no sense of God's presence ? There may be examples of this, though we are safe in judging that they are few. But some such failure is thoroughly consistent with the point we have been making. It is not maintained that the conditions mentioned, such as quietness and humility, are *sufficient* conditions of a sense of God's presence, but, in general, *necessary* conditions. They are preparations *without which* we cannot expect to see God, but this is not to say that those who follow them will always see God. The spirit, we are told, bloweth where it listeth. There is still an unpredictable element about the highest experiences ; certainly they cannot be made to order.*

* This general problem is handled with philosophical skill and religious feeling by the Archbishop of York. See William Temple, *Nature, Man and God*, op. cit., pp. 398-403.

B.   Lack of Sensory Quality

A second difficulty, which seems to stand in the way of more than a few, arises from the fact that religious experience is not sense experience. We know we are dealing with reality, so the argument runs, as long as we can find the weight of an object or measure its length. If only we can secure a photograph we are reasonably sure that we are not deluded by ascribing reality to what is only imaginary. God must be imaginary because he is not known by any of our senses ; God has the same status then as the " object " of a dream which is purely subjective.

A considerable part of the difficulty thus felt arises from the ambiguity of the word " sensation ", and is dispelled by the effort to give it a precise meaning. What are we asking when we ask whether a religious experience is sensory ? If we mean, Is there any sense organ for religious experience, as there is for visual experience ? we can only answer that there is none, so far as we know. The whole man seems to be involved. But if by sensation is meant vivid awareness, especially of what is experienced as objective, then it is sensory. A number of people in our time appear to accept the narrower meaning and hold that the " sense " of God is illusory because it has no known physical counterpart.

Perhaps people cannot be dislodged from this naïve sensationalism if they are deeply prejudiced in its favour, but we can at least point out that the position has nothing other than prejudice to commend it. How can men possibly know that their only contact with what is real (in the precise sense given above of independent existence so far as observation is concerned), is by means of certain end organs of their bodies? After all, these end organs are nothing but instruments which catch and transmit certain messages of external origin. There is a conspicuous difference between ether waves and the experience of sound, and the whole matter is so mystifying that dogmatic assertions are manifestly out of place. The miracle by which physical events pass over into mental events is just as much a miracle as ever, when we have ascertained that this must take place through the instrumentality of the brain. If it be said that knowledge *without* the use of end organs is too wonderful, the adequate reply is that it is quite as wonderful *with* the end organs. If we follow the method of science we do not decide in advance that non-sensory knowledge is illusory, but we start with experience and if we have a great weight of testimony in favour of experience which is both indubitable and non-sensory, we must make a consequent enlargement of our notion of how experience comes. It is ridiculous to rule out religious experience on *a priori* grounds, but that is precisely what the sensationalist does.

We can go farther, however, than an argument for the possibility of valid non-sensory experience; we can point to accepted examples of it in other

fields than religion.* Perhaps the most satis-
factory example is that of mathematical insight,
which is a well-attested experience. The history
of mathematical discovery is, to a large degree,
an account of what men have learned without
necessary reference to what comes by way of the
eyes and ears. Not only are there conceptions
which have no counterpart observable by the
senses, but many of the important discoveries
have been made by men with " their eyes shut ".
Sometimes these discoveries are such that sense
experience can be employed later to verify them.†

Another piece of evidence consists of the fact
that most people claim to have a certain amount
of self-knowledge, but they would hardly go so
far as to hold that all of it comes by way of the
senses. It is somewhat difficult to see, for
example, how a man's knowledge of his own
conscientious scruples could be brought to him
by the aid of sensory end-organs. We know other
persons partly by their bodies, but a mere
knowledge of their bodies does not carry us far.
Those interested in this particular argument
should consult the work of Professor Webb, who,
after a careful consideration concludes :

> In no case is the fact of sense-perception taken by
> itself the ultimate court of appeal as to the real existence

* It should be made clear that we are making no reference
here to the experiments in what has been recently called
" Extra-Sensory Perception ". Our contention does not
stand or fall on the success of such experiments.

† This paragraph has been written with the help and
advice of able mathematicians.

whether of oneself, of another person, or even of an external object ; and one therefore certainly cannot take it as the ultimate court of appeal in the case of the existence of God, since God is, according to those most concerned to assert his reality, not an object of sense even in the way in which another person may be said to be such.*

Denial of reality to what is not apprehended by the senses would be as fatal to art as to religion. Artistic creation is a matter of making visible or audible to others what the artist has already glimpsed in a non-sensory way. The history of artistic production shows conclusively that " the light that never was on sea or land " is not sheer verbiage. We might conceive of a world in which all these phases of experience are left out, but it would be a meagre, dull world, and we can hardly have an adequate world view if we beg the question of the nature of reality in advance. " Philosophy, in framing its conception of the universe ", says Professor Milburn, " must take account of every order of facts within it."†

It is reasonable to expect that, in a world which includes different orders of facts, there should be different ways of knowing those facts, each order having its appropriate method. In that case, the fact that one area of reality cannot be known as is another is not an argument

* C. C. J. Webb, *Religion and Theism*, George Allen & Unwin Ltd., 1934, pp. 104, 105.

† R. Gordon Milburn, *The Logic of Religious Thought*, London, 1929, p. 25.

against it. Thus physical things are known
largely by sense perception, values by contempla-
tion, and persons by sympathetic insight. Why
make one the test of others? We shall not do so
if we have a keen sense of the complexity and
variety of the world order.

C. Lack of Describable Content

A third difficulty in many minds concerns the
lack of content in religious testimony. Those
who see a tree can tell a great deal about it, and
thus prove that they have really seen it, but
those who report religious experience seem to tell
very little. They have certainty, indeed, but
sometimes it seems like nothing more than
certainty of certainty. If men have known God
why cannot they tell us in sober prose what God
is like? Instead of doing this they seem, to the
outsider, to indulge in vague, rhapsodical, and
meaningless talk.

Much of this difficulty is overcome when we
realize that religious experience is like aesthetic
experience in that it is concerned more with
appreciation than information. On the highest
levels, information about the object seems beside
the point, for we are lost in wonder.

Sometimes we wish there were more content
in such experiences, more information given, but,
upon second thought, we realize that there are
levels of communication, even between finite
persons, far higher than those which involve

information.   In a great crisis we ask of another, not news, but something very old, an assurance that the relationship, of love or friendship as the case may be, still remains.   The sense of assurance is far more important than is a message in which the chief element is descriptive.   A great many of the letters which people await so eagerly all over the world have either no new information in them, or trivial information, but they are prized because they tell again a well-known story.

Furthermore, there is a true sense in which any experience is ineffable ;   we cannot explain it to those who have no intimation of it at first hand.   We cannot explain colour to the congenitally blind, who feel that all our talk about colour is vague, rhapsodical and meaningless.   An academic neighbour of mine tried once to tell a group of students about the *joys* of study, but he found that they laughed.   This sense of the joy of study was ineffable ;   they did not understand or even believe that an experience such as he described was possible.   If this is true in such a commonplace effort, there does not seem to be much point in ridiculing the saints for their inability to make others understand.

That ineffability of experience leads directly to poetry and symbolism, Dean Inge has been tireless in showing :

Language, which was framed to express daily needs and common ideas, breaks down when it is called upon to describe the deeper experiences of the soul.   It struggles to find similes for what cannot be said directly.

If the poet, and sometimes the artist—William Blake, for instance—are driven to use strange symbols to express their ideas, personifying the forces of nature and hunting everywhere for metaphors and analogies, even more must this be so with the religious genius.*

There is, of course, an ancient and honourable way out of the problem of ineffability, the way so beautifully demonstrated by Plato in the *Meno*. We cannot give people any understanding of what they totally lack, but we can *remind* them of what is implicit in their lives. Religious experience is not *really* ineffable. All have some fleeting experiences to which we can appeal and by means of which they can be made to understand. There is good reason to believe that congenital blindness does not occur in the life of the spirit.

D. *Religious Wish Thinking*

A fourth problem is presented by the fear, very widely and justly felt, of the colouring of our testimony by our desires. The little child wants a particular kind of playmate so badly that he invents one and talks about him in sober terms. Perhaps, in spite of the strong evidence for the experience of God, all this is a testimony to man's wistfulness rather than to anything in the objective order. Perhaps God is the adult's " Imaginary Playmate ".

Those who have read Professor Gilbert Murray's justly famous essay, " Stoicism ", will remember

* W. R. Inge, *Studies of English Mystics*, pp. 18, 19.

the note of haunting sadness with which it ends. He sees philosophy after philosophy come finally to the assertion of the reality of a " Friend behind phenomena ", but he resists the tendency to suppose the assertion is, for that reason, in accordance with truth. Perhaps the conviction only demonstrates our yearning, perhaps it rests, not on observation, but upon almost ineradicable instinct, a yearning for what is not there. What if religion should be nothing more than " the groping of a lonely-souled gregarious animal to find its herd or its herd-leader in the great spaces between the stars " ?

Men have long been aware of the danger of " wish-thinking ", realizing that hopes may be liars, but certain developments in modern psychology have greatly emphasized the danger, especially by the device of providing a special jargon, which has passed into popular speech. By some we are taught the extreme doctrine that all beliefs are dictated by instinctive urges. Because religion is concerned with those things about which people have greatly cared, it has seemed an easy mark for this kind of analysis.

This characteristic argument against the assumption of objective reference in religious experience is well summarized by Dr. Sigmund Freud, in his small book, *The Future of an Illusion*. Men, so the argument runs, having first idealized their fathers and then having discovered that their fathers are not the strong, just beings they supposed, have turned to a world of phantasy where they project the ideal father image on a cosmic screen. Being unable to bear the hard reality of disillusionment, men escape from reality, and worship the projection their own desires have made.

There is little use in beating the ghost of Freud, since the glaring logical lapses of his position have been pointed out by so many. We may, in passing, however, show that the chief weaknesses of Freud's position are the following two. First, his doctrine proves far too much. Why does it not follow that all scientific conceptions are likewise projections? Men, sick of disorder, have perhaps fastened on the illusion of an ordered cosmos. Apparent verifications of astronomical predictions are then wish fulfilments. Furthermore, on this basis, why is not Freudianism itself suspect? What irrational desires make the Freudian present his doctrines, including that of the illusory character of religious experience? That which rules out everything rules out none.

The second glaring weakness lies in the fact that Freud is engaged in a stupendous process of question begging. Religion, the psycho-analyst tells us, is an escape from the real world, this escape being dictated by the desire to find a firm foundation on which we can depend. *Because* it is an escape, it is illusory. But this assumes, in advance, that we know what reality is, else how can we escape it. Now this question of the nature of the real is the very point at issue. In any case this can hardly be decided without reference to the testimony of religion according to which certain clear claims about the nature of the real are made.

" The whole attack ", Professor McDougall points out, " amounts to saying that man's nature is such as naturally leads to the development of religions, therefore religion is purely illusory."* The original proposition is correct, but the second does not follow from it. That our nature leads us to be religious is not, alone, a convincing argument for the validity of religion, but neither is it an argument against it. What we desire *could be* true. We can sympathize with the present Dean of St. Paul's when he hopes " it is not disrespectful to say that the majority of psycho-analysts seem to suffer from a defective general education ".†

One phase of the problem concerning religion and wishful thinking, which many seem to overlook, is found in the fact that religious experience has often been at complete variance with men's desires. It has been found in all generations that religion has made men uncomfortable, driving them to almost superhuman sacrifice. " What doth the Lord require ? " is, as we have seen, a characteristic question. Man connects his religion in every generation, not with what he wants, but with his conception of what he ought to be and

* William McDougall, *Psychoanalysis and Social Psychology*, London, 1936, p. 54.

† W. R. Matthews, *Essays in Construction*, London, 1933, p. 22.

do. This is conspicuously true of prophetic religion which is based, more largely than most, on direct experience. It is really difficult to see how any thoughtful person can lightly ascribe religious experience to wish thinking in the face of the tremendous and abiding fact of the Cross. " It is hard to understand ", as Dr. Buttrick so pointedly says, " why mankind should have created a fiction-God who demands sacrifice : it would have been so much easier in a heartless world to have taken painless poison."*

One of the strongest evidences of the non-illusory character of religious experience lies in this very tendency to apprehend God as One who is independent of our desires and even our expectations. From the time of Xenophanes we have repeated the clever quip that men make God in their own image. This is a partial truth which gives a distorted view of the actual situation. It may indeed be true that the Orientals picture their divinities as slant eyed and the Ethiopians theirs as snub-nosed, but these are the external features of mere representations. The deeper truth is that men have so often, and especially in times of spiritual awakening, recognized in God something utterly different from themselves, something that *judges* themselves. " My ways are not your ways, nor My thoughts your thoughts, saith the Lord." The ascription of perfection to God is a clear indication of the opposite tendency

* George A. Buttrick, *The Christian Fact and Modern Doubt*, New York, 1935, p. 72.

to that which Xenophanes wittily but superficially observed.

In the same way it is untrue to maintain that religious experience always mirrors the prevailing teaching, in such a way that experience may be accounted for by expectation. In the history of religion, especially in prophetic periods, experience denies the current teaching and cannot be considered as fully dependent upon it. Inasmuch as the Hebrew prophets, with their immediate sense of God's leadership, denounced so many of the received ideas, it is futile to suppose that what men are taught is a sufficient " explanation " of religious experience. Too often the language of religion is : " Ye hath heard it said, but I say unto you."

Not only does the content of religious experience frequently run counter to what men have been taught to expect, but the experience itself sometimes comes to men when they least expect it. We do well to emphasize expectancy as part of the mood which makes men receptive, but we must beware of stressing it in such a way as to suggest that something like self-hypnosis takes place. We help to restore balance when we remember men who, like St. Paul, have seen the living Christ, not when they expected it, and certainly not when they hoped for it, but in opposition to all their hopes and expectations.

It is often claimed that religion may be " traced to " a sense of human helplessness. We may justly inquire the meaning of " traced to ".

Does this mean that the sense of helplessness, perhaps a left-over of childhood, is a necessary condition of religious experience or a sufficient condition ?   Manifestly it is not the latter, since many who have it report no experience of God. If a necessary condition is meant, is not the proposition merely a repetition of what religious men have long said, especially about the necessity of the child spirit ?

The fact that an experience can be " traced to " one situation, does not mean that it may not, with equal validity, be traced to several others at the same time.   My vision of the sunset may be traced to the fact that I have eyes, but it may also be traced to the fact that there is a sun to observe, and that no wall intervenes.   The conditions which are requisite to the total experience are really extremely numerous.

Professor James Bissett Pratt has done much to clarify this aspect of the question by his illustration of the imaginary race in which the human organism is always bathed in light as in an Arctic summer.   Most of the people are blind, but a few see.   One of these seers, who constantly receives light sensations when his eyes are open is investigated by the psychologists.   They find a correlation between raised eyelids and light sensations.   " Light sensations ", they conclude, " are the invariable accompaniment of open eyes ; they are, in fact, a ' function ' of open eyes."   No reference thus need be made to the sun or any external source.

The naïve seer, innocent of the ways of science, might indeed insist that he saw the *sun*, and not merely his own sensations ; but the psychologist would assure him that he mistook his sensations for something objective, that, in fact, he was substituting interpretation for description, and that the only verifiable and scientific fact was his sensations of light.*

Professor Pratt does not tell us what the seer said at the end, but we are justified in supposing he laughed heartily. In other words a psychological description is useful and important, but we are making a leap of thought when we infer from a psychological account the necessary denial of objective reference. In conversion there may be interesting psychological " laws " demonstrated and these may include the unconscious, but this does not rule God out. " In conversion ", writes Bennett, " the deeps of the soul are stirred. True. But it is also possible that an angel may have troubled the pool."†

The removal of these objections sets us free to accept the general fact of religious knowledge at its face value, using the test of agreement here, as in other levels of experience, to distinguish between the illusory and the real.

* J. B. Pratt, *The Religious Consciousness*, New York, 1924, pp. 457, 458.

† C. A. Bennett, *The Dilemma of Religious Knowledge*, p. 109.

IV

VERIFICATION

And although the arguing from experiments and observations by induction be no demonstration of general conclusions yet it is the best way of arguing which the nature of things admits of, and may be looked upon as so much the stronger, by how much the induction is more general.

SIR ISAAC NEWTON.

IN the modern use of the scientific method, investigators have placed, and rightly placed, the emphasis on verification. No matter how reasonable a proposition may appear, those who belong to the Newtonian tradition are not satisfied until its truth has been verified. In this, scientists are not deterred by a recognition of the logical difficulty that verification rests upon what is actually a formal fallacy, since all verification is the " affirmation of the consequent ". We reason that " If x is true, y is true ", and then, having found y true a great many times, we proceed to the affirmation of x. It is easy to see how fallacious such reasoning may be in single cases. Consider the simple illustration of an alleged earthquake. We know that, if there is an earthquake, houses tremble. Our house trembles, therefore there has been an earthquake. Such an affirmation of the consequent is quite likely to lead us astray since there may have been other situations productive of the trembling of the house, such as the passing of a heavy load on the street or an explosion of dynamite.

In scientific method we do not deny that such reasoning back from effect to cause is fallacious, but we recognize that in practical experience it is the only way we *can* reason, and we reduce the likelihood of erroneous conclusions by testing a great variety of effects in a great variety of places. If the trembling of our house is matched by trembling of distant houses, including those far away from both highways and explosives, and if this evidence is matched by abundant observation of other effects, all consistent with the original hypothesis, we say the occurrence of the earthquake is verified. *We overcome a fallacy by committing it in sufficient amount.* Such scientific reasoning does not give absolute proof, but it gives as much proof as anyone wants. We have it on good authority that our sole evidence for the existence of atoms is of this character. If there were atoms, then certain effects would be observable. Since these effects are actually observed we conclude that atoms exist even though *they* are never immediately perceived. The evidence grows as the verification proceeds.

In view of the conviction which verification produces it is fair to ask whether religious experience can be verified. Can we make some check on what men claim to know when they report a sense of God's presence ? When an astronomer claims the experience of seeing a hitherto undiscovered planet, other astronomers direct their telescopes to the point where the alleged planet is supposed to be and thus they verify the observations of the discoverer. Until this is done we rightly remain somewhat sceptical.

The essence of verification is the repetition of the original observation or experiment to see whether the alleged results follow. Perhaps the results were achieved in the first case because of some peculiar element in *that* situation ; by trying the same operation in a new situation we may eliminate much of the possibility of illusion. We repeat the performance and watch for the repetition of effects.

When acting upon the hypothesis leads one into experiences in which what is supposed in the original hypothesis becomes a fact of first-hand experience, this is working which amounts to verification.*

It will be seen that verification is merely a specialized form of the test of agreement and, therefore, much of what appears in Chapter II of this Lecture shows the way in which the objective reference of religious experience has been verified. The saints and prophets have reported the wonderful discovery that God manifests himself to men when they open their eyes in a special way. In generation after generation other men proceed to open their eyes in this way and, though not all of them report

* D. C. Macintosh, *The Reasonableness of Christianity*, New York, 1925, p. 22.

the sense of God's presence and saving power, the number who do so is so great that the combined power of their testimony is almost overwhelming. As scientist checks scientist, so saint checks saint. The objective character of Augustine's experience is verified by its fundamental repetition in the life of Pascal.

In all verification, regardless of the employment of " objective methods ", we are never able to eliminate dependence upon human testimony, since all that we know arises in experience, and it is people who have the experiences. Therefore the character and dependability of men who testify to any fact are of paramount importance. Popular beliefs concerning many scientific questions rest on faith in the reliability of a mere handful of men who are qualified to know, men who could perpetrate a gigantic hoax if they chose to do so. What they *are* makes us trust what they *report*. Frequently, in connection with alleged historical events, we have no other basis of dependence than the capacity of certain men to inspire trust. A consideration of polar discovery is illuminating in this regard.

Admiral Peary, according to his well-known account, reached the North Pole on April 7th, 1909, in the company of five other men. How can we be certain that this occurred ? We cannot fail to realize that, had he been an impostor, he could have taken advantage of the technical ignorance of the four Eskimaux and one Negro who accompanied him. Of course Peary took pictures, but one Arctic scene looks very much like another.

It must be remembered that this question of the actuality of alleged Polar exploration is not a merely academic one. When Peary returned he was amazed to learn that Dr. Frederick A. Cook claimed to have sledged to the pole the year previous to Peary's arrival. Which man was to be believed? No doubt practically all who consider the matter now believe Admiral Peary rather than Dr. Cook, but their reasons depend primarily on the general character and reputation of the men. In the same manner our verification of religious experience is facilitated by the trust which men of character and intelligence, such as Augustine and Pascal, engender. Since we cannot, in spite of our scientific mood, eliminate the personal equation, we are correct in stressing the personal qualifications of those who give testimony. This phase of the question sheds new light on the immense importance of the experience of Jesus Christ.

Though in the historical report of religious experience we are forced to rely on the character of men, the desirable features being a combination of honesty and the critical spirit, the situation in religion is such that we have an added check. Religious evidence is more closely parallel to evidence in astronomy than to evidence in history. What we seek to verify is the objective reality of God, as known in religious experience, and this reality continues, as does a scientific object, whereas an historical event is forever gone.   In religion we have a two-fold basis of evidence, the trustworthiness of those who have testified in the past, and the possibility of the experimental knowledge of God here and now.   This immediate verification is open to every sincere and devout person, for though the conditions are rigorous, they do not include the esoteric.

A great part of what we call scientific method lies not so much in the actual technique of experimentation as in the ability to plan novel experiments which will verify an hypothesis in some new and unsuspected manner.   Though we do not seek to manipulate men, we can at least observe what happens in novel situations that might be expected to check our alleged religious fact in a new way.   On this account we have waited eagerly for Admiral Byrd's account of his experiences during the time that he was alone in the Antarctic waste for so many months in 1934. Since all realize that there is at least a portion of truth in Professor Whitehead's dictum that religion is what a man does with his solitariness,* it might be expected that *real* solitude would open a man's eyes to spiritual reality in an unusual way.   In a situation like that of Admiral Byrd of the Antarctic, a man ought to know God if he ever would, for a man is then removed from the thousand and one distractions which so often confuse our sight.

* Alfred North Whitehead, *Religion in the Making,* Cambridge, 1926, p. 16.

Many readers of Admiral Byrd's book, *Alone*, must have watched eagerly for the revelation of his inner experiences, and they have not been disappointed in their expectation. The explorer tells us that the experiences are so personal that it took four years for him to bring himself to the point where he could publish the account. When Byrd went to the " Advance Base ", he was not at all what we ordinarily mean by a religious man, if we may judge by his own record,* but he welcomed the entire freedom from interruption because he wanted time to think. To his surprise, he came away convinced of the reality of what we have called the presence of God. Under the date of April 14th, he wrote in his diary :

The day was dying, the night being born—but with great peace. Here were the imponderable processes and forces of the cosmos, harmonious and soundless. Harmony, that was it ! That was what came out of the silence—a gentle rhythm, the strain of a perfect chord, the music of the spheres, perhaps.

It was enough to catch that rhythm, momentarily to be myself a part of it. In that instant I could feel no doubt of man's oneness with the universe. The conviction came that that rhythm was too orderly, too harmonious, too perfect to be a product of blind chance—that, therefore, there must be purpose in the whole and that man was part of that whole and not an accidental offshoot. It was a feeling that transcended reason ; that went to the heart of man's despair and found it groundless. The universe was a cosmos, not a chaos ; man was as rightfully a part of that cosmos as were the day and night.†

* He admits, for example, that he was habitually profane.
† R. E. Byrd, *Alone*, New York, 1938, p. 85.

Then, on June 2nd, came the entry which helps
to make the title of the book doubly significant :

The human race, then, is not alone in the universe.
Though I am cut off from human beings, I am not
alone.*

When most people ask whether religious
experience can be verified they apparently mean
that they want something as convincing as is a
photograph in astronomical study. The significance of the photograph lies in the fact that the
existence of the object reported has *made a difference*, in this case the difference being the change
of a camera plate or film. We correctly ask,
" Was some permanent mark left, a mark which
others may see ? " When no such effects can be
shown, the fact may be as it is asserted, but it is
not verified, and we are justifiably sceptical.

In religion we cannot reasonably look for a
mark on photographic plates, but we can reasonably look for a mark on human lives. If the
experience of God is what men claim it is, we
should expect to see a general change in their
character ; we should expect them to walk with
a new step. It is this that we can check
abundantly in a way that should be convincing
to the open-minded. The evidence of altered
lives, including both new strength and new
tenderness, is so great that only a small portion
of it has ever been committed to print. Not all
of those who have reported religious experience

* Ibid., p. 183.

have demonstrated " the fruits of the spirit ",
but, in considering evidence of this kind, we are
concerned not so much with what is universal as
with what is typical. We can show the typical
verification through moral strength, by pointing
to characteristic experiences in different settings.

In presenting the fruits of the spirit as evidence
of the truth of the basic religious claim we are by
no means adopting a merely pragmatic conception
of the meaning of truth. There are in the world
untruths that are morally efficacious, at least for
a time. We do not hold that all things which
" work " are true, but rather that those which
are true may reasonably be expected to " work ".
When, therefore, we point to the moral efficacy of
religious experience we are not presenting a
conclusive proof, but are engaging in precisely the
same " affirmation of the consequent " on which
all scientific verification depends and which
approaches proof as the body of the evidence
increases, especially under a variety of situations.
The effects of religious experience do not stand
alone, but are part of the cumulative proof,
according to which the problem is approached
from several angles at once.

There have been some lives in which the access
of power following upon a strong sense of the
revelation of God is so great as practically to make
our questionings seem impertinent. Such a life
was that of Sadhu Sundar Singh. In regard to
his greatest religious experience, in which he was
fully awake and in the midst of his normal life,

Sadhu Singh had not the slightest doubt of the reality of objective reference. C. F. Andrews writes in his admirable biography :

This objective character of the incident was always insisted upon by him, however much others might seek to weaken his evidence, or try to prove to him that it might have come merely from his own excited imagination. He would strongly assert that the difference between an inner vision of the mind and this outward appearance was absolute. He alone could give the final proof in such a matter, and he had offered that proof in its most convincing form by living an entirely different life—so changed, that he had been obliged to face suffering, hardship, persecution, and even death itself, for Christ's sake. He had done so with joy and gladness.*

In considering an account so searching, especially in view of the sequel in this man's life, the normal response is to doubt whether a purely subjective experience could work such wonders in a man so alert.

If it be said that the case of Sadhu Sundar Singh is an isolated case, we can turn to a movement in which such an access of power may be illustrated by an entire people faced with persecution. The story of the rise of Quakerism in the middle of the Seventeenth Century provides one of the most exciting and revealing chapters in the history of the human spirit. Literally thousands of otherwise inconspicuous people were subject to two experiences, the first being a

* Charles F. Andrews, *Sadhu Sundar Singh*, London, 1934, p. 73.

vivid sense of the immediate revelation of God, and the second being unflinching courage in the face of bitter persecution. It was the conviction of these thousands that there was a direct causal relationship between these two experiences, and the modern reader, as he reviews the evidence in its abundance, can avoid the same conclusion only with the greatest difficulty. Just as it is hard to account for the transformation of the first Christians into an aggressive group, except on the hypothesis that the experience at Pentecost was what it seemed to be, so it is hard to account for the transformation of Yorkshire dalesmen into spiritual heroes except on a similar hypothesis.

The most searching reading concerning the early Friends is that which recounts the sufferings of Friends at the hands of their enemies. The story comes to us with overwhelming effect as we peruse the faded pages of *New England Judged*, or *The Sufferings of the Quakers*. The first of these, written by George Bishop, and published as early as 1661, includes on its title page the following description :

Wherein the cruel whippings and scourgings, bonds and imprisonments, beatings and chainings, starvings and huntings, fines and confiscation of estates, burning in the hand and cutting of ears, orders of sale for bond-men, and bond-women, banishment upon pain of death, and putting to death of those people are shortly touched.

As we read the old pages we get a glimpse of what must have gone on in the minds of men who lay in prison in Boston, Massachusetts, far from their families and friends, awaiting death by hanging, and yet sustained by an abiding sense of God's presence. One of these, Marmaduke Stevenson, wrote a paper, after he had received his sentence of execution, which is already taking its place among the classic expressions of religious experience :

In the beginning of the year 1655, I was at the plough in the east parts of Yorkshire in Old England, near the place where my outward being was, and as I walked after the plough, I was filled with the love and presence of the Living God, which did ravish my heart when I felt it ; for it did increase and abound in me like a living stream, so did the love and life of God run through me like precious ointment, giving a pleasant smell, which made me to stand still. And as I stood a little still, with my heart, and mind stayed on the Lord, the word of the Lord came to me in a still small voice, which I did hear perfectly, saying to me, in the secret of my heart and conscience, *I have ordained thee a prophet unto the nations ;* and at the hearing of the word of the Lord, I was put to a stand, being that I was but a child for such a weighty matter. So at the time appointed Barbadoes was set before me, unto which I was required of the Lord to go and leave my dear and loving wife and tender children. For the Lord said unto me immediately by his Spirit, that he would be an Husband to my wife, and as a Father to my children, and they should not want in my absence, for he would provide for them when I was gone. . . . So in obedience to the Living God, I made preparation to pass to Barbadoes in the 4th month 1658. So after some time I had been on the said island in the service of God, I heard that New England had made a law to put the servants of the Living God to death, if they returned after they were sentenced away, which did come near me at that time ; and as I considered the thing, and pondered it in my heart, and did not declare it to any until the time

appointed . . . and for yielding obedience to, and obeying-
the voice and command of the Everlasting God, which
created heaven and earth, and the foundations of waters,
do I, with my dear brother, suffer outward bonds near
unto death.   And this is given forth to be upon record,
that all people may know who hear it, that we came not
in our own wills, but in the will of God.*

Comment on such an account is superfluous.
We can only say that if this be illusion, how grand
is illusion !

A similar verification of the reality of religious
experience, as shown in its power to produce a
joyous spirit of overcoming, took place in countless
English prisons as well as in Massachusetts.   One
of the most appealing of these records is that of
Francis Howgill, who was a resident of Stevenson's
neighbouring county, Westmorland.   Howgill, one
of the strongest of the leaders who allied themselves with George Fox when he went to the
north of England in 1652, was imprisoned for
several years in Appleby Gaol, where he was at
the mercy of a cruel and unscrupulous gaoler.
He died in gaol in his fiftieth year, about ten
years after Stevenson was hanged in Boston.
George Fox's " Testimony concerning Francis
Howgill " makes the situation vivid :

They committed him to Appleby Gaol in the year
1664, and there they kept him from sessions to the

* The testimony appears in Bishop's *New England Judged*,
1661, pp. 107-8.   It is found also in Besse's *Sufferings*, 1733,
Vol. I, pp. 508-10.   It is easily available to the modern
reader in *Christian Life, Faith and Thought in the Society of
Friends*, pp. 32-4.

assizes in a smoaky hole, and at last they premunired him ; and his body being almost spent in the service of the Lord, being a weak man, there did he offer up his life, as a sacrifice for his faith for the Lord Jesus Christ's truth, and died a prisoner for the name of Jesus in the latter end of the year 1668 and so laid down his life as a testimony against the persecutors.*

A few months before he died Howgill wrote " An Epistle to the Flock of Christ ", which reveals both his strength, in spite of physical weakness, and the source of that strength. In this he said :

God by his Holy Spirit gives daily hints of his love in the inward man unto all stayed minds, and assurance of the victory, which makes me often overlook present suffering, and forget the afflictions that are past, and little to heed present things, though they seem to frown, because the Light of God's countenance is lifted up, and his favour, and love, and strengthening power felt in the inward man, which balances all, and weighs down the scale of present trouble and affliction, so that hard things are become easy, and ponderous things light.†

Were not Howgill and Stevenson verifying one another's conclusions ?

In the midst of his last sickness Howgill said that he was content to die, and that he was ready, and praised God for those many sweet enjoyments and refreshments he had received on that, his prison-house-bed, whereon he lay freely forgiving all who had a hand in his restraint.‡

* Found at the beginning of Francis Howgill's *Works*, called *The Dawnings of the Gospel Day*, 1676.

† Ibid., p. 734.

‡ Ibid., Introduction.

When we consider such experiences it is not surprising that the representative executive body of the Society of Friends in England is called the " Meeting for Sufferings ".   A generation ago it must have seemed to many that this ancient name was quaint and almost meaningless, but the turn of events in our day has made the old language contemporary once more.   There was a time when the hangings on Boston Common seemed incredibly remote ;   we could with difficulty believe such accounts.   But now these stories have a modern sound.

There has come out of Germany a little book of letters written by imprisoned pastors which, when translated into English, sounds wonderfully like the record of the sufferings of Seventeenth Century Friends.   Even the title, " Und Lobten Gott " could be used in either case, for did not Francis Howgill tell how he praised God in prison ? In letters like these, where we see the human soul stripped of all its normal human aids, we get what is perhaps the most convincing evidence of the objective reality involved in religious experience that the world can offer.   The Foreword* to these remarkable letters tells us in clear words what the experience is that sustains these men :

Many among the writers with only a slender measure of physical health and nervous strength would, especially

* More than one English translation has been made.   I am using that of my colleague, Miss Helena Dye, of Stanford University.   The Student Christian Movement has brought out a translation called *I was in Prison*.

as fathers of a family, not be able to write as they do if the living Christ were not present with them as the most real of all realities.

It would also be wrong if a reader in the reading of these pages should come only to the conclusion : " Yes, here men are standing up for their convictions." However much it may appear to human understanding to be that, in reality there is something infinitely greater here than merely a subjective conviction. It is the living Christ, to whose reality these pages bear witness.

We have not space here for many of these documents, but the two following will suffice :

I cannot tell you how thankful I am for the inner experience I have been permitted to have in these days. Though I walk through the valley of the shadow, I fear no evil, for Thou art with me. This presence of God in such a situation becomes even now a precious reality. And how good it is that our faith may now manifest itself really as faith, not merely in words, but in deeds and in the attitude in which we stand ready to take upon ourselves unpleasantness for the sake of the faith, if God thus permits it that men oppress us for our faith's sake. No one will be able to say any more what formerly in foolishness was sometimes said : He merely talks that way because he is paid for it. . . .

God's ways are wonderful. And where he leads through dark ways, there one experiences his glory most. And again and again the experience is repeated : " You thought to bring evil upon me, but God thought to turn it to good." I am sure that all this, too, which we are now going through will serve " only more for the further-ance of the gospel " in our congregation, without the congregation's needing to get into unwise (imprudent or reckless) agitation if our church services are forbidden.

God has thrown us Christian people in our church to-day out of all safe nests, out of all the nests of earthly security and human calculations and plans, cast us out

as it were into emptiness, into nothingness. In sudden
shock and terror we may have felt sometimes in these
years as if we were plunging into a bottomless abyss,
sinking away into nothingness. What are we now to
do ? Now we must *fly* if we do not want to be borne
away by the storms of oppression into the yawning
chasms of despair. But if we only really learn to *believe*,
yes learn *really* to *believe* in God, and in firm belief and
trusting prayer spread our wings, then we shall experience—and how many times in these years we have
already experienced it with amazement and awe—that
we do not sink away, there is a power there which holds
us, we are borne by God's eternal father-arms, we are
sustained in the storms.

What can we say in the face of testimonies
so tremendous ? Words seem impertinent and
silence the only adequate response. If that
which sustains men and makes them praise God
in such dark hours be not reality, where is reality
to be found ? In the sustaining power of the
living God we have a message which is at once
timely and timeless, timely because it is needed
now as perhaps never before, and timeless because
it appears in identical form when men are forced
to turn away from all which normally makes
them feel secure, yet fails them in an emergency.
It has been proved repeatedly that one Resource
does not fail. It is in this combination of the
timely and the timeless that verification occurs.

We have stressed these two examples of
persecution and sustaining power, not because the
objective quality of religious experience is chiefly
shown in such situations, but because we have
in these examples the possibility of verification

in a striking manner. Since the same general conditions are repeated in a new setting, and with new experimenters, in a new century, we watch to see whether the expected results do actually occur. The fact is that they do. But we should be making a grave mistake if we should conclude from this that the only verification comes in times of dramatic strain. The verification takes place daily and hourly in millions of inconspicuous lives. As humble individuals we may not add the slightest item to the store of wisdom, but each one can share in the exciting and never-ending process of verification. The communion of saints is another name for " The Fellowship of Verification ".